195
Y0-CKH-407

# THE PURIM

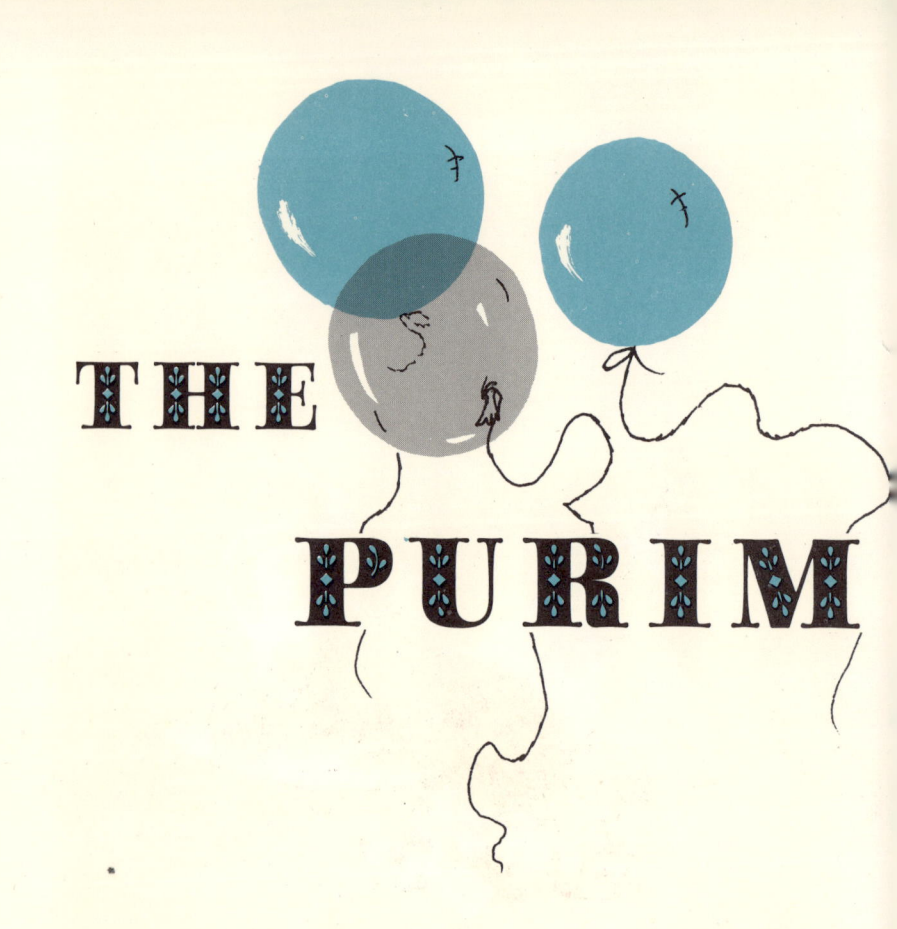

*by* Norma Simon

*illustrations by* Ayala Gordon

סְעוּדַת פּוּרִים

# PARTY

United Synagogue Commission on Jewish Education

Copyright © 1959 by United Synagogue of America · Printed in U.S.A.

Good Yom Tov! Good Yom Tov!
Today's the Purim Party!
When will Grandma come?
I want to wear my costume.

Who will you be, David?
Will you be Mordecai?

I will be the queen.
Her name is good Queen Esther.
Let's *gragger* with our *graggers,*
   the way we did last night.

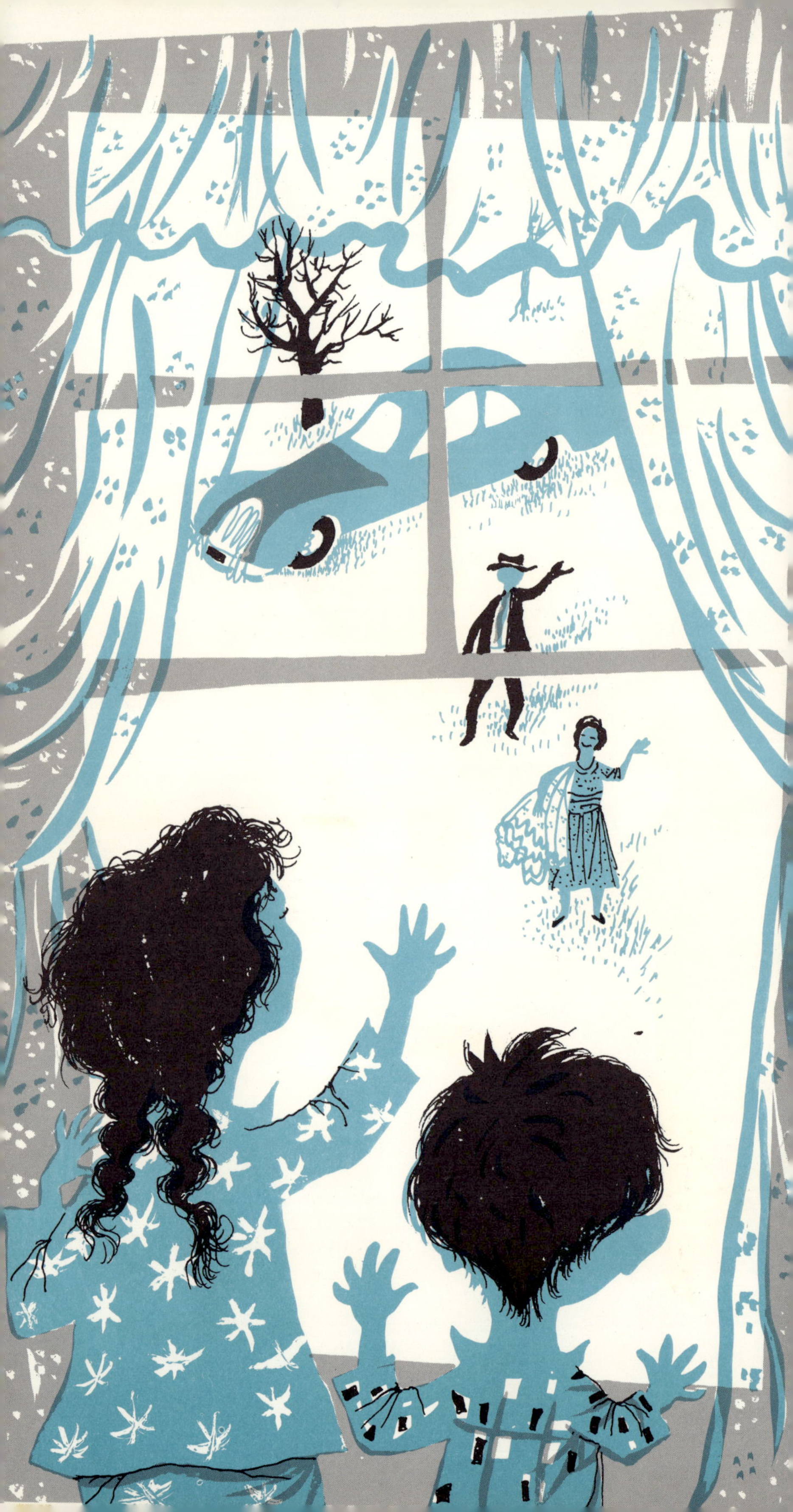

Here comes Grandma.
Here comes Grandpa.
They're coming out of their car.
*Good Yom Tov!*
*Good Yom Tov!*
Let's hurry and get dressed.


Grandma, Grandma,
I can hardly stand still.
I want to look in the mirror.
I want to see me change
    into good Queen Esther.


Did you make the veil
    for under my eyes?
It must be hard to eat and drink
    wearing a veil.
Don't you think?

When I grow up, and I'm a grandma,
    will I know how to sew?
I want to make costumes, too,
    just like you.

Why is David's costume like a dress?
Is that like Mordecai?

Did men wear long gowns long ago?
Now they all wear pants.
You look different, David,
    like a picture in my book.
I like the way we look,
    like people long ago.

Grandpa will drive us
  In his shiny new car.
  I will see my friends,
    like people long ago.

*Good Yom Tov!*
*Good Yom Tov!*
I saw you all last night.
We all *graggered* with our *graggers*
    when we heard the *Megillah*.
*Gragger gragger gragger gragger*
    every time we heard "Haman."

Who are you, Joel?
Who are you, Susan?

Who are you, Daniel?
My grandma made my costume.
Who made yours?
Did you bake *Hamantashen*?
Did you buy *Hamantashen*?
Which kind do you like best?

I like poppy seed,
and I like prune.

They're both so good.
It's hard to choose.

We have a parade,
 parade of all the costumes.
 All in line across the stage.

ELI

SUSAN

JOEL

DAVID

DANIEL          ME

AND ALL THE CHILDREN

SLOWLY MARCHING

SLOWLY MARCHING

MAKING THE PURIM PARADE.

We dance around in a circle.

We sing our Purim songs.

We eat our *Hamantashen*.

We *gragger* with our *graggers*.

We laugh.

We talk.

Happy Purim Party.

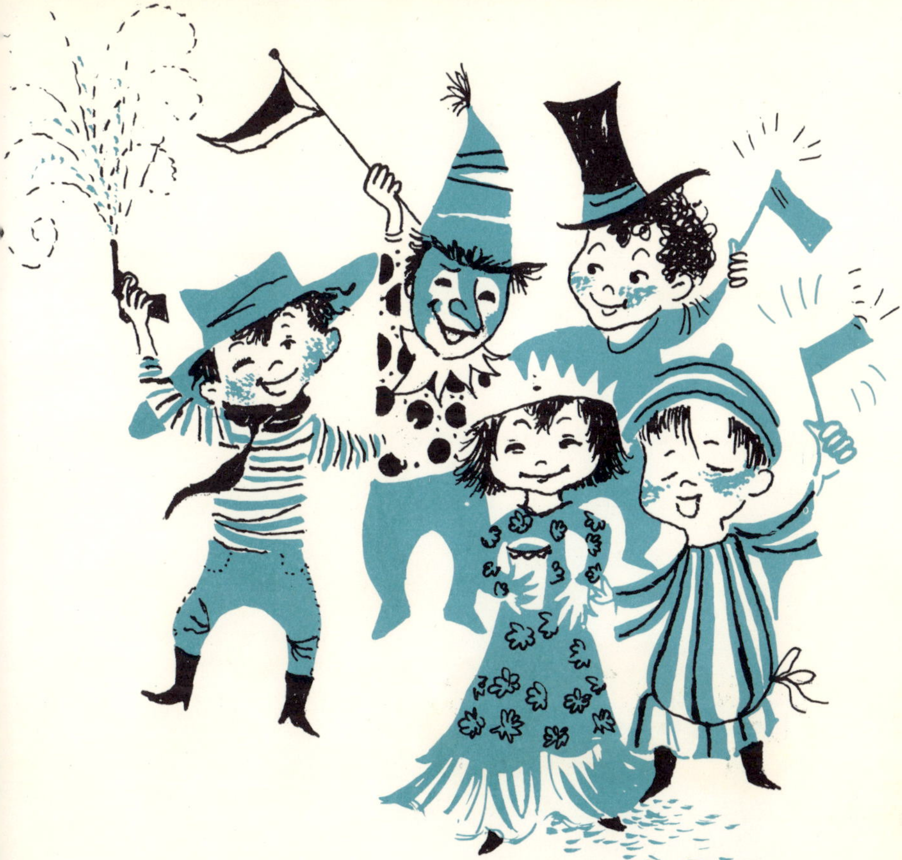

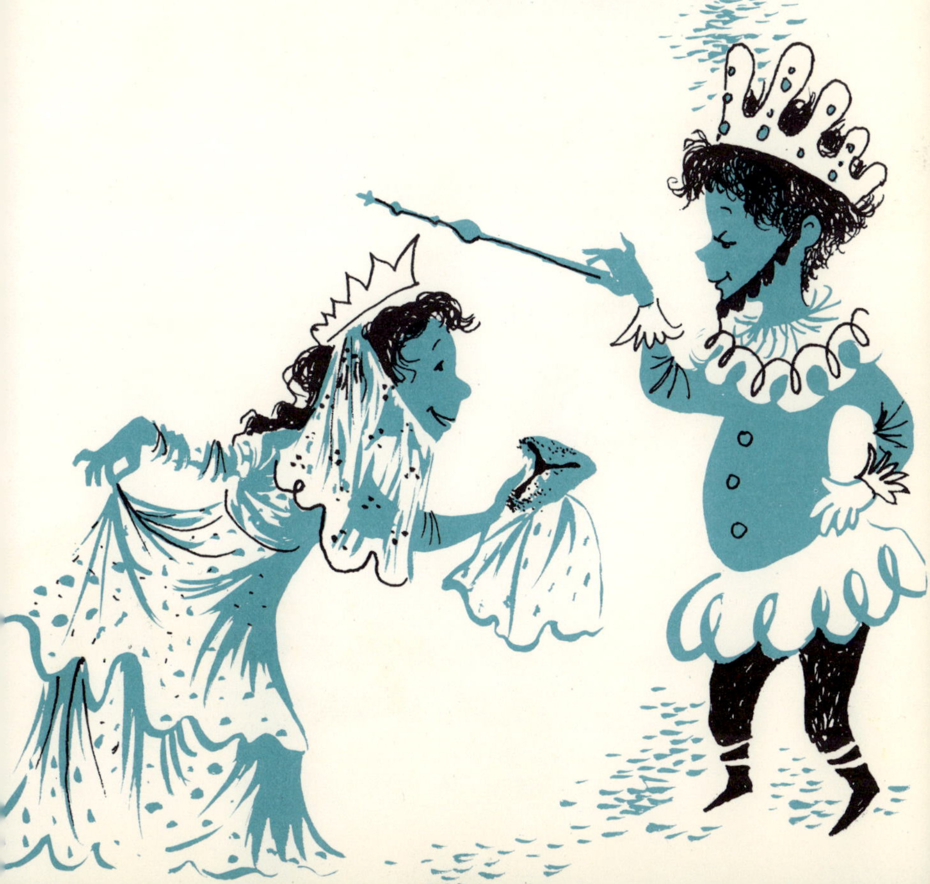

Home to dinner
>	a very special dinner.
Home to the *S'udah*
>	a Purim Party dinner.
I stay in my costume.
David is Mordecai.
I pretend to be a queen
>	and hold my *gragger* high.

The family sits around.
Grandpa starts remembering.
Daddy starts remembering
>	many other Purims a long time ago.
Grandpa tells a story
>	about when he was a little boy.
Daddy tells a story
>	about when he was a little boy.

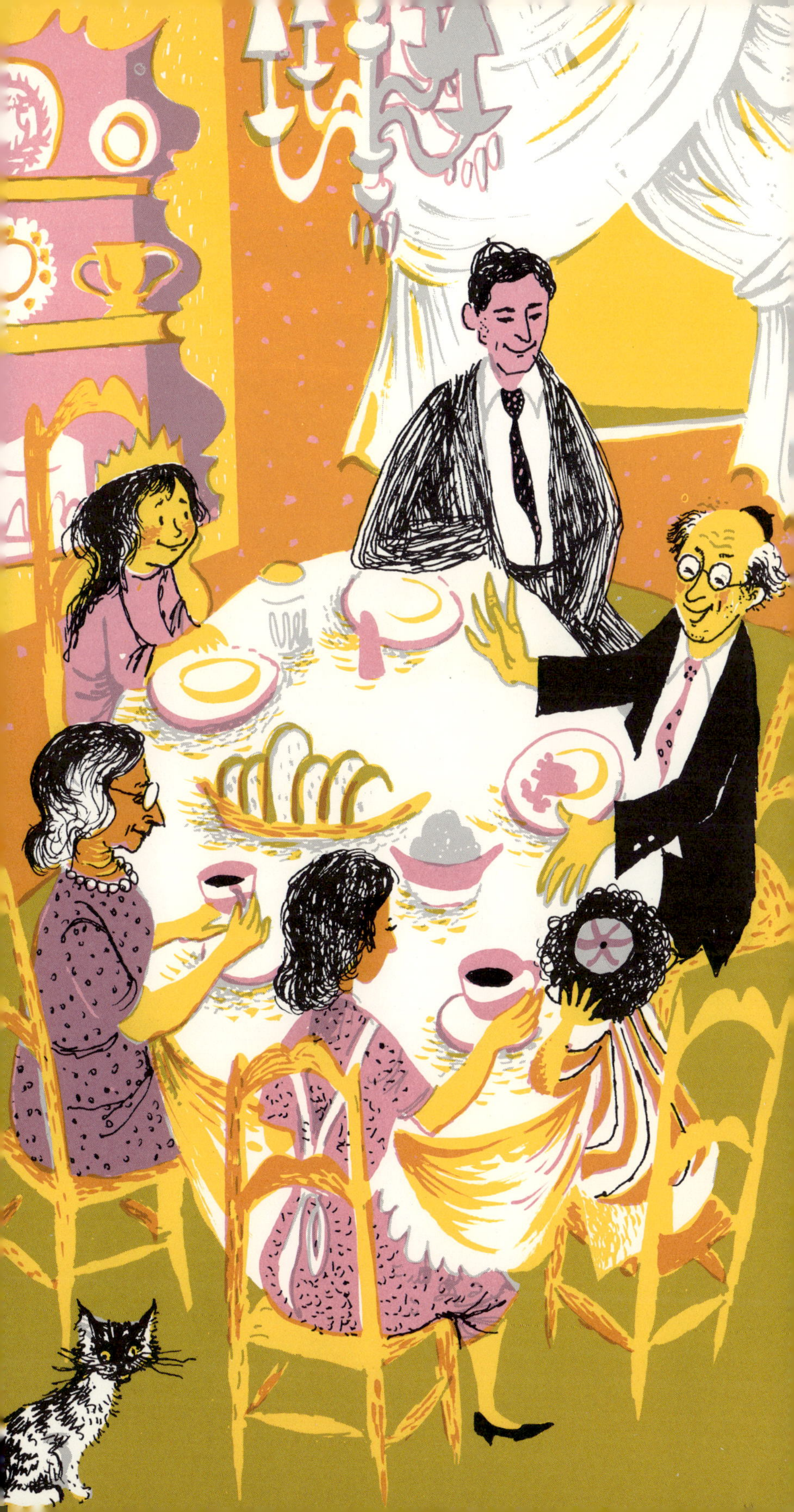

Grandpa goes out to the trunk of his car, the place he keeps surprises.

He says, "A present for Ruth,
  a present for David, too,
    presents for both my grandchildren,
    presents for both of you."

Daddy takes out presents.
Daddy hands them out.
"One for good Queen Esther,
 one for Mordecai.
Open your presents, children,
 while Mother brings in our dessert."

Mother brings in a plate of *Hamantashen*.

Prune for David.

Poppy seed for Grandpa.

Prune for Grandma.

Poppy seed for Daddy.

Poppy seed for Mother.

Poppy seed for me.

Enough for everybody.

I take a little taste of prune,
      and a little more poppy seed.
Another year, next year.
More *Hamantashen!*
    More *Megillah!*
        More *graggers!*
           More Purim!

**NOTE TO PARENTS AND TEACHERS**

The words *Gragger, Gragg Gragg Gragg, Hamantashen,* and *Good Yom Tov* can be substituted by their corresponding Hebrew words if the situation demands it. The words would be *Ra'ashan, Rash Rash Rash, Oznei Haman,* and *Ḥag Same'aḥ*.

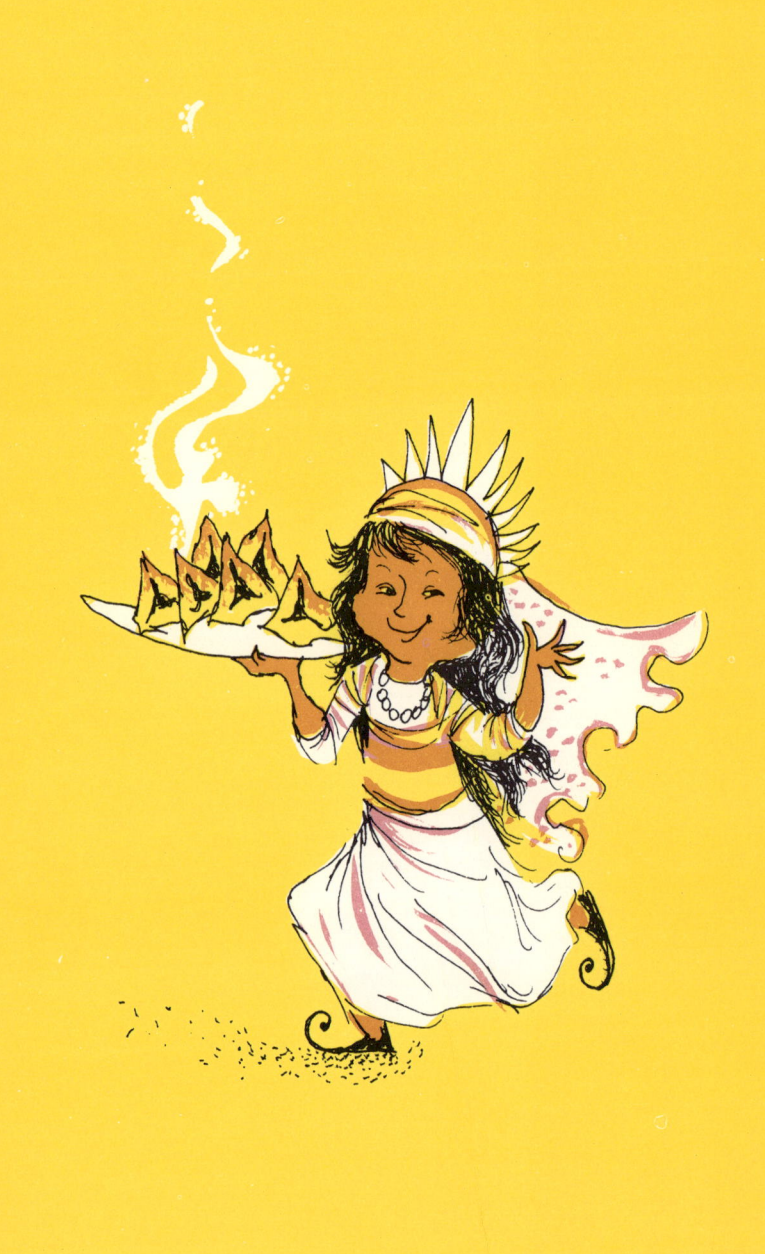